T0276305

Quintessential Knits for baby

whimisical knits for little ones

20 hand knit designs for newborn - two years

Judith Quinton

TATE PUBLISHING
AND ENTERPRISES, LLC

This title is also available as a Tate Out Loud product. Visit www.tatepublishing.com for more information.

Published by Tate Publishing & Enterprises, LLC
127 E. Trade Center Terrace | Mustang, Oklahoma 73064 USA
1.888.361.9473 | www.tatepublishing.com

Tate Publishing is committed to excellence in the publishing industry. The company reflects the philosophy established by the founders, based on Psalm 68:11,
"The Lord gave the word and great was the company of those who published it."

Book design copyright © 2014 by Judith Quinton.
Cover and interior design by Judith Quinton
Illustrations by Judith Quinton

Published in the United States of America

ISBN: 978-1-63449-630-8
1. Crafts & Hobbies / Needlework / Knitting
2. Crafts & Hobbies / General
14.08.19

This book was inspired by the anticipated arrival of
Aria Lyn.

When word came that you were on your way,
I looked for the perfect item to knit for you.

When the picture in my mind
couldn't be found on any bookshelf,
I decided to take that picture and knit it.
This is for you,
my beautiful inspiration.

Contents

Introduction 6

Knitting Tools... 8

How-To... 11

Glossary 18

Hats...23

    Pixie Party Hat 26

    Beanie...30

    Berry Bliss Hat 32

    Aviator Hat 36

    Strawberry Cupcake Hat 40

    Parisienne Bebe Slouchy 42

    Fancy Faerie Hat.. 46

    Play Date Hat 48

    Goin' Fishin' Bucket Hat............................. 52

    Girls' Day out Cloche 54

    Pageboy Hat 58

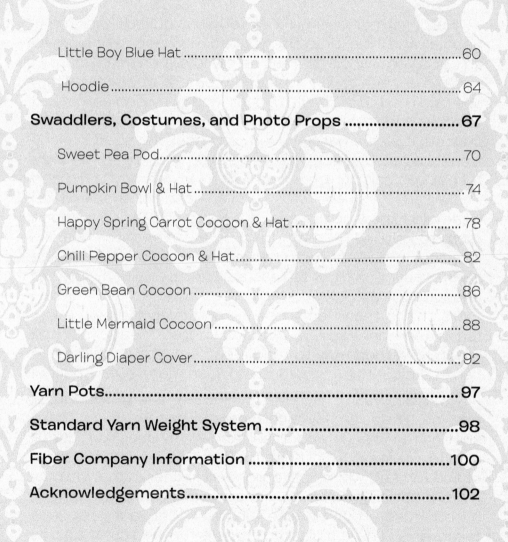

Little Boy Blue Hat 60

Hoodie 64

Swaddlers, Costumes, and Photo Props 67

Sweet Pea Pod 70

Pumpkin Bowl & Hat 74

Happy Spring Carrot Cocoon & Hat 78

Chili Pepper Cocoon & Hat 82

Green Bean Cocoon 86

Little Mermaid Cocoon 88

Darling Diaper Cover 92

Yarn Pots 97

Standard Yarn Weight System 98

Fiber Company Information 100

Acknowledgements 102

Introduction

Watching my Mom knit socks on what looked like so many needles and little, tiny stitches had me wanting to learn to knit at a very early age. Imagine my joy when she thought I was old enough to learn! After a moment of despair when she said I had to start with a scarf and two needles instead of socks and four needles, I quickly moved on, eager to get started. It was a passion from day one! The scarf making frenzy began. One of my brothers even challenged me with, "I'll bet you can't finish a whole scarf in one day!" I did and immediately thought I was such an accomplished knitter! Little did I know at the age of eight that there was much more to knitting than whipping up a garter stitch scarf in less than a day. My mom had taught me to knit, but she hadn't taught me how to read a pattern, so when I was old enough I got a book and learned for myself. After knitting more things than I could count and overwhelming every family member with my glorious knitted creations, I had not only learned how to read a pattern, but I could make cables, knit in the round, and so much more. I was hooked!

Over the years, my love for knitting has grown into a passion to design. My eight-year-old self wants to make knitting fun while my adult self knows my designs must fill a need. Quintessential Knits for Baby is a coming together of the fun and whimsical childhood knitter in me with my more practical adult side. I hope you find the patterns in my book useful but more so, fun to knit! Let your inner child takeover and have a blast. Knitting is fun, and creating this book was, too. Enjoy!

Judith Quinton

All my life, mom has been crafting things—sewing, painting, scrapbooking, crocheting, photography, and knitting—if it's something creative, she's probably tried her hand at it. Being truly an artist at heart, she loves nothing more than sharing her passion and passing her knowledge on to others.

Through the years, my sisters and I have gone from watching to being the (usually willing) recipients of some mighty-fine teaching in many of mom's creative pursuits. Who we are today has much to do with the hands-on creative upbringing we were so lucky to have. We grew up drawing and painting, taking photos (I had my first camera before I was two years old), and making things from mom's yarn and fabric scraps, rarely realizing that we were learning just by trying to follow in her footsteps. In this age, when you can go online and buy anything for a deal, we still love to make things—beautiful, hand-made creations. And, yes, we both knit, though not nearly as much as our mom. I actually have no idea how one human being knits that much!

Now, she will have a new generation to pass these things along to, the first grandbaby in the family being the reason for this most recent outpouring of creativity. She has truly put so much of herself into this book, I hope you enjoy reading it and trying your hand at the patterns as much as I know she enjoyed creating them. And, if you get the chance, pass along your love of knitting—or anything creative for that matter. It's one of the best gifts you could give, except for maybe one of the adorable goodies you're about to see inside these pages!

From our family to yours, we hope you find something you will love to make, love to give, love to pass on. Now, let's get knitting!

Annie (Sisters: Katelyn and Kayla)

{ Knitting Tools }

Circular needles

Crochet Hook

Double Point Needles

Measuring Tape

Scissors

Stitch Holder

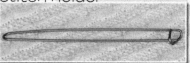

Stitch Markers

Straight Knitting Needles

Tapestry Needle

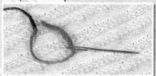

{ How-To }

Casting on

Begin with a slip knot.

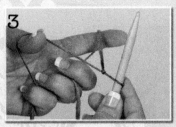

Hold yarn as shown with the tail over your thumb and the ball yarn over your finger.

Insert needle as shown under the yarn.

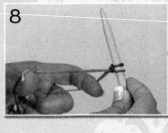

Bring needle over the yarn on the 1st finger as shown and pull it back through the two strands on the thumb as shown in photos 5, 6 and 7. Let the yarn go to form a knot on the needle as shown in photo 8. Continue this until you have the required amount of stitches cast onto the needle.

Knit Stitch
(Throw Method)

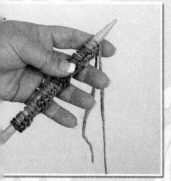

This is what your needle looks like after casting on.

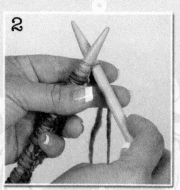

Insert needle as shown behind the cast on (or left) needle.

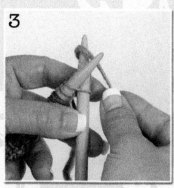

Wrap yarn around from back to front.

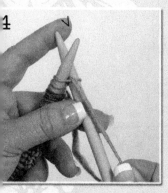

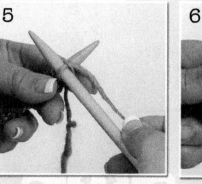

Holding yarn with right hand, slide the needle down the back of the left needle then bring to front between first and second stitch as shown in photos 4 and 5.

Slide new stitch off the left needle leaving it on the right needle as shown in photo 6. The first knit stitch is complete.

Purl Stitch

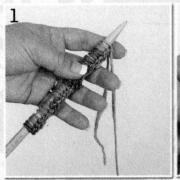

1

This is what your
needle looks like
after casting on.

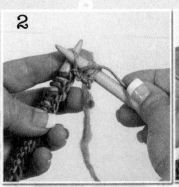

2

Insert needle as shown
in front of the cast
on (or left) needle.

3

Wrap yarn around from
back to front over
the right needle.

4

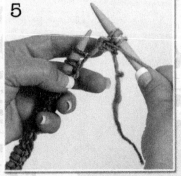

5

Holding yarn with right hand, slide right needle
down the front of the left needle and to the back
(the opposite of knitting) as shown in photo 4.

Slide the new stitch off the left needle
leaving it on the right one as shown in photo
5. The first purl stitch is complete.

Binding Off

Knit the first stitch as shown in photo 1. Knit the second stitch as shown in photos 2 and 3.

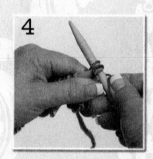 

Insert needle into first knit stitch as shown in photo 4, and pull it over the top of the other stitch and off the end of the needle, leaving only one stitch on the needle. (photos 5,6 and 7) Repeat from Step 2 until only one stitch is left. Then, cut yarn and thread it through the last loop.

Making a Pompom

Wrap yarn around your three fingers (or a piece of cardboard) the required number of times according to pattern (shown in photos 1, 2, and 3)

  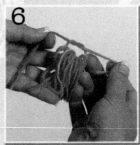

Slip a piece of yarn through all loops as shown and tie a square knot (shown in photos 4, 5 and 6).

Pull yarn tight (image 7). You have made what I call a "Loopy Pompom." If you want a more traditional look, after you have attached it to the hat, cut the loops as shown (shown in photos 9 and 10).

Stockinette Stitch

The stockinette stitch is made in the round by knitting every row. If working a flat piece, it is made by knitting a row then turning your work over and purling the next row,

Garter Stitch

The garter stitch is made in the round by knitting a row then purling a row. If working on a flat piece, knit every row.

Ribbed Stitch

The ribbed stitch is made by alternating a knit stitch and a purl stitch. In a 1x1 rib (shown here in brown) you would knit one then purl one. You can also make 2x2 by alternating two knit stitches with two purl stitches. This stitch is usually used for cuffs, as well as any edge that should be more form fitting.

Glossary

Abbreviations

"	inch (es)
( )	work instructions between parentheses, in the place directed
BO	bind off
CC	contrasting color
CO	cast on
Dpn	double pointed needle(s). A short needle with points at both ends
K	knit
K2tog	knit 2 stitches together
M1	make 1. This means to increase a stitch.
P	purl
P2tog	purl 2 together
Pm	place marker
rib	ribbing, as in (K1, P1) ribbing
sl st	slip stitch(es)
st (s)	stitch(es)
tog	together

Terms

Binding off – To finish your project you must get the stitches off your needle.

Casting on – The first step in all knitting projects, this is how you get stitches onto your needle.

Decrease – To reduce the number of stitches you have on your needle. Decreasing is often required for shaping a garment, such as making an armhole of neck hole. There are several different methods of decreasing, but the most popular is knitting (or purling) two stitches together.

Garter Stitch – A basic knitting pattern in which every row (in flat knitting) is knit. In circular knitting, you knit one row and purl the next. It looks the same on both sides. This is the most basic pattern in knitting

Increase – To get more stitches onto your needle in the middle of a pattern, an increase is needed. The most basic way to increase is knitting in the front and the back of a stitch.

Knit stitch – The knit stitch is the most basic form of knitting. You slip the needle into the loop from front to back, then loop the working yarn around that needle, slide the stitch through to the front and slide off onto the other needle.

Knit two together - Knit two together is the most basic method of decreasing.

Make one - This is a way of increasing stitches. It is when you either knit in the front and the back of a stitch (making two from one) or knitting the "bar," which is the yarn between the stitches.

Long Tail Cast On - Long tail is a method of casting on that uses both ends of the yarn to cast the stitches onto the needle. It's called this because of the long tail of yarn you pull out of the ball in order to make the stitches. You need to make sure you pull out enough yarn or you will run out before all your stitches are cast on. Once you get the hang of it, it is fast and simple. It also makes kind of a stretchy edge.

Purl Stitch - Purling is often called the opposite of knitting. This stitch is formed by inserting the needle from back to front instead of from front to back. The working yarn is in front instead of in back when the stitch is made.

Stitch Markers - Stitch markers are little, round items, usually made of plastic or metal that can be slipped onto the knitting needle to mark a certain place in a row. Stitch markers are used to mark the end of a row in circular knitting, so you don't lose track of where the row ends. They can also be used to mark where increases and decreases are.

Stockinette Stitch - A basic knitting pattern where the first row is knit and the second row is purled when you are knitting flat. If you are circular knitting, you will knit every row. The "front" side of the fabric will look smooth while the back will look bumpy.

{ Hats }

Pixie Party Hat

Chunky Rolled Brim Beanie
(hers and his)

Berry Bliss Hat

Aviator Hat

Strawberry Cupcake Hat

Pariesienne Bebe Slouchy

Fancy Faeire Hat

{ Hats }

Play Date Hat
(his and hers)

Goin Fishin' Bucket Hat

"Girls Day Out" Cloche

Pageboy Hat

Little Boy Blue Hat

Hoodie
(his and hers)

{ Pixie Party Hat }

Materials

Yarn:

MC Lanaloft bulky weight
Color - Turquoise Magic
CC - Ozark Handspun
Color - Star Child

Needles:
US size 15 straight
US size 17 straight

Etc.
Stitch marker
Tapestry needle

Finished Size:
Newborn: 13–14" head
6 -12 months: 16"
18-24 months: 18"

This hat warms their sweet little head and looks fabulous doing it! Easy to knit on large straight needles, it works up fast. The handspun fiber trim adds some fun to the party!

BODY:

Using size 15 straight needles and MC, cast on 12 (14, 16) stitches. Leave a 10" tail of yarn at beginning for ties.

Row 1 and all odd rows: Knit

Row 2 and all even rows: Purl

Work until piece measures 11(13, 15) inches, ending with a knit row. Bind off knit wise leaving a 10" tail for ties.

Using size 17 needles and CC, with right side facing you, pick up every stitch on long edge of piece, leaving a 10" tail for braided ties (this should be along the side that has two 10" tails that will be used later for ties).

Row 1: Knit

Row 2: Purl

Bind off loosely, purl wise. Leave a 10" long tail for braiding.

With tapestry needle and MC, sew back seam. Work in ends.

TIES:

Cut 2-20" long pieces of CC
(one for each braided tie)

Cut 2-20" long pieces of MC
(one for each braided tie)

Loop one strand of each color through
the end at the front of the hat.

Using three strands held together, braid
to desired length and tie a knot.

Cut tails to be the same length.

LOOPY POM POM:

With both colors held together,
wrap them around a 2 1/2" piece
of cardboard (I used three fingers
instead) about 16-20 times and cut.

Using a strand of MC, tie a knot
around the strands to form a pom
pom (see how-to with photos on
page 19). Don't cut. Attach it to the
point on the top of the hat.

{ Beanie }

Materials

Yarn:
MC Malabrigo Gruesa
Color - Lettuce
CC - Elsebeth Lavold Silky Wool
Color - Mild Green

Needles:
US size 17 straight
or dpn's

Etc.
Stitch marker
Tapestry needle

Finished Size:
Newborn: 13-14" head
6-12 months: 16"
18-24 months: 18"

Beanies always seem to be in style, and why not? They are comfy and look great! Make it perfect for your little one's head by using this super soft, thick and thin, self-striping fiber mixed with silk wool. Hmm... Maybe it's time to go make one in my size!

BODY:

Using size 17 circular needles, holding both MC and CC together, cast on 28 (32, 36) stitches. Join and knit in the round. Knit every row. Work until piece measures 4½ inches (5 ½, 6 ½)

SHAPING CROWN:

Switch to dpn's when needed.

Row 1: (K2, K2tog) around

Row 2: Knit

Row 3: (K1, K2tog) around

Row 4: Knit

Row 5: K2tog around

Row 6: Knit around

Cut yarn, leaving a 6" tail.

Using a tapestry needle, thread yarn through remaining loops. Bring yarn to inside and finish off.

Berry Bliss Hat

Materials

Yarn:
MC   Malabrigo Gruesa
Color – Buscando Azul
CC   Jewel Fiber Design
Color – Green

Needles:
US size 13 – 16" circular
US size 17 – 16" circular & dpn's

Etc.
Stitch marker
Tapestry needle

Finished Size:
Newborn 13–14" head
6–12 months 16"
18–24 months 18"

What a berry sweet way to top any little head, not to mention how soft and comfy it is! This knits up quick and easy, so it's great to make and take as a last minute gift for that special little someone!

BRIM:

Using size 13 circular needles and CC,
cast on 30 (34, 38) stitches.

Place marker and join to work in the round.

Rows 1-6: Knit

BODY:

Change to MC

Row 1: (K6 (8, 9) M1) around stitches
(for two larger sizes, end with K2)

Row 2: Knit

Rows 3-9 (3-11, 3-13): Change to size 17 needle and knit.

DECREASE:

Newborn size

Row 10: (K3, K2tog) around

Row 11: Knit

Row 12: (K2, K2tog) around

Row 13: Knit

Row 14: (K1, K2tog) around

Row 15: Knit

Row 16: K2tog around

Row 17: K3tog, K3tog, K1

Rows 18-20: Using dpn's K3 rows of i-cord

Finish off.

6-12 month size

Row 12: (K17, K2tog) twice

Row 13: (K4, K2tog) around

Row 14 and all even rows: Knit

Row 15: (K3, K2tog) around

Row 17: (K2, K2tog) around

Row 19: (K1, K2tog) around

Row 21: K2tog around

Row 23: K2tog around

Rows 23-25: Using dpn's K3 rows of i-cord

Finish off.

18-24 month size

Row 14: (K5, K2tog) around

Row 15 and oll odd rows: Knit

Row 16: (K4, K2tog) around

Row 18: (K3, K2tog) around

Row 20: (K2, K2tog) around

Row 22: (K1, K2tog) around

Row 24: K2tog around

Row 26: K2tog around

Rows 27-29: Using dpn's K3 rows of i-cord

Finish off.

Aviator Hat

Materials

Yarn:
MC Cascade Yarn
Jewel Hand Dyed
Color - 9887 Brown
CC 1   Color – Off white
CC 2   Color – Black

Needles:
US size 15 straight needles
Crochet Hook size H

Etc.
Stitch marker
Tapestry needle

Finished Size:
Newborn 13–14" head
6–12 months 16"
18–24 months 18"

For your little Amelia Earhart or Charles Lindbergh this hat is fun for any occasion! Soft fibers and earflaps make it warm and functional too. If you can't crochet there is an alternative goggle technique at the end of this pattern. Enjoy!

HAT:

Using size 15 straight needles and MC,
cast on 32 (36, 40) stitches.

Rows 1-8 (10,12): Knit

Row 9 (decrease row): (K6(7,8), K2tog) across

Row 10 and every even row: Knit

Row 11: *K5(6,7), K2tog* across

Row 13: *K4(5,6), K2tog* across

Row 15: *K3(4,5). K2tog* across

Row 17: *K2(3,4), K2tog* across

Row 19: *K1(2,3), K2tog* across (continue to decrease in
pattern for two larger sizes)

Row 21: K2tog across

Leaving an 8 inch tail (for hat seam), cut yarn. Sew back
seam using a tapestry needle.

EARFLAP: (Make 2)

Leaving front 12 stitches open pick up and knit 6 (8, 10)
stitches for earflap.

Rows 2-6: Knit

Row 7: K2tog, K2 (4, 6), K2tog (continue to decrease in
pattern for larger sizes by k2tog at each end of row)

Row 8: Knit

Row 9: K2tog twice.

Row 10: Knit

Row 11: K2tog, finish off.

EDGING:

With CC1 and using crochet hook, sc in each stitch around entire hat and earflaps.

GOGGLES:

With CC2 and crochet hook, sc 6stitches in a magic ring (check out online instructions http://ambassadorcrochet. com/2012/02/14/how-to-make-a-crochet-magic-ring/).

Sl st to beginning sc.

Ch1, sc in same stitch. 2 sc in each st around, join with sl st.

Ch1 sc in same st, 2 sc in each st around, join to ch st and tie off. (Make 2)

For the largest size, I do another row of sc's around.

With CC1, attach to circle with sl st, ch 1 and sc in each st around, join with sl st to beginning st. 2 dc in next st (nose strap) then sl st to join second circle. Sc in each st around the circle join with sl st to beginning sc. Tie off.

To make strap ch 34 (38, 42). Dc in 3rd ch from hook and in each around. With tapestry needle and CC1, sew goggles to hat.

For an alternative to crocheting the goggles: Cut circles from black felted wool. Cut larger circles and a strap from off white felted wool. Blanket stitch the circles together and to the strap. Attach the strap to the hat by blanket stitching with off white.

Strawberry Cupcake Hat

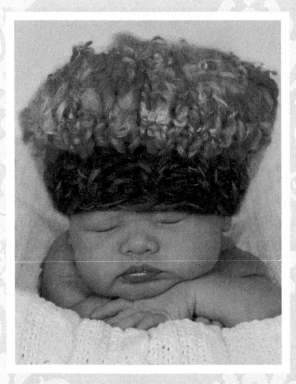

Materials

Yarn:
MC   Ozark Handspun
Color – Strawberry
CC   Cascade Jewel thick-n-th
Color – brown

Needles:
US size 13 – 16" circular
US size 17 – 16" circular and dpn's

Etc.
Stitch marker
Tapestry needle

Finished Size
Newborn 13-14" head

A great gift idea or as a fun addition to baby's first portrait session, this cupcake hat is just an all-around fun addition to baby's wardrobe. If you use the yarn mentioned above it even smells like strawberries!

BRIM:

Using size 13 circular needles and with MC, cast on 22 stitches.

Place marker and join.

Work in (K1, P1) rib for 1 ½".

Next row: (K5, M1) around (26sts)

BODY:

Change to size 17 circular needle and CC.

Row 1: (K5, M1) around.

Rows 2-7: Knit

Row 8: (K11, K2tog) around

Row 9: (K4, K2tog) around, K1

Row 10: (K3, K2tog) around, K1

Row 11: (K2, K2tog) around, K1

Row 12: (K1, K2tog) around, K1

Row 13: K2tog around

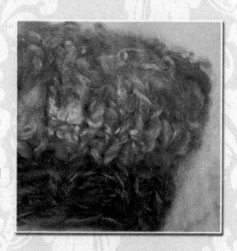

Using tapestry needle, thread yarn through remaining loops and finish off.

Parisienne Bebe Slouchy

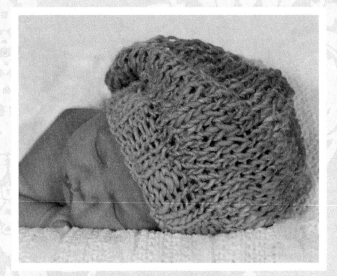

Materials

Yarn:
MC   Noro silk cotton
Noro Silk Garden
Color Rainbow #87

Needles:
US size 10 – 16"circular
US size 13 – 16" circular
& dpn's

Etc.
Stitch marker
Tapestry needle

Finished Size:
Newborn 13-14" head
6-12 months 16"
18-24 months 18"

This stylish slouchy hat is a lightweight addition to baby's wardrobe. Great for any season! The silk cotton yarn by Noro is self-striping so you get a gentle transition from one color to the next.

BRIM:

Using Size 10 circular needles and MC, cast on 40 sts.
Join in the round and work in (K1, P1) rib for 5 rows.

BODY:

Change to size 13 needles.

Row 1: Knit

Row 2: (K5, M1) around (48 sts)

Row 3- 10 (or desired length): Knit

DECREASE:

Newborn size

Row 11: (K6, K2tog) around

Row 12 and 14: Knit

Row 13: (K5, K2tog) around

Row 15: (K4, K2tog) around

Row 16: (K3, K2tog) around

Row 17: (K2, K2tog) around

Row 18: (K1, K2tog) around

Row 19: K2tog around

Cut yarn leaving a six inch tail. Using tapestry needle, thread yarn through remaining stitches and finish off.

6-12 month size

Row 11: (K7, K2tog) twice
Row 12, 14, 16, 18: Knit
Row 13: (K6, K2tog) around
Row 15: (K5, K2tog) around
Row 17: (K4, K2tog) around

Row 19: (K3, K2tog) around
Row 20: (K2, K2tog) around
Row 21: (K1, K2tog) around
Row 22: K2tog around.
Finish off.

18-24 month size

Row 11: (K8, K2tog) around
Row 12, 14, 16, 18, 20: Knit
Row 13: (K7, K2tog) around
Row 15: (K6, K2tog) around

Row 17: (K5, K2tog) around
Row 19: (K4, K2tog) around
Row 21: (K3, K2tog) around
Row 22: (K2, K2tog)
Row 23: (K1, K2tog) around
Row 24: K2tog around
Finish off.

{ Fancy Faerie Hat }

Materials

Yarn:
MC   Jewel Hand Dyed
Color – Dark Salmon
CC   Ozark Handspun
Color – Star Child

Needles:
US size 13 – 16" circular & dpn's

Etc.
Stitch marker
Tapestry needle

Finished Size:
Newborn 13-14" head
6-12 months 16"
18-24 months 18"

Everyone needs a bit of fancy and this hat has it! Using the jewel hand dyed fiber gives it a great texture, while the Ozark Handspun adds some fun.

BRIM:

Using size 13 circular needles and MC, cast on 90 (102,114) stitches

Row 1: Knit

Row 2: K2tog around

Row 3: Knit

Row 4: (K1, K2tog) around 30 (34, 38) stitches remaining

BODY:

Turn work and Knit every row (in the round) for 14 (18, 22) rows.

Next row: Purl around (to form ridge, see image 1)

Changing to dpn's when needed, continue as follows:

Row 1: K2tog around

Row 2: K around

Row 3: K2tog around

Row 4: K around

Row 5: K2tog around

Row 6: K around

Row 7: K2tog around

Row 8: K around

For a longer point, K i-cord for a row or two.

Finish off.

FOR HAT BAND:

With size 13 circular needles and CC, pick up 30 (34, 38) sts where the brim and body meet (as seen in photos). Knit one row then bind off.

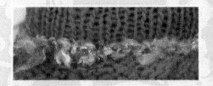

{ Play Date Hat }

Materials

Yarn:
MC Mini Mochi
(or any worsted weight yarn)

Needles:
US size 13 - 16" circular & dpn's

Etc.
Stitch marker
Tapestry needle

Finished Size:
Newborn 13-14" head
6-12 months 16"
18-24 months 18"

This simple hat is made to work for boys or girls. While the body of the hat remains the same for both, the pompoms and ties can be changed.

HAT:

With size 13 circular needles and MC,
loosely cast on 28 (32, 36) sts.

If you knit tightly, you will need to add 2 sts so you will cast
on 30 (34, 38) depending on the size you are making. Join
to work in the round.

Knit every row until piece measures 7 (9, 11) inches.

If you choose to make a stripe in this hat (as shown in the
pink version below), just knit row 6 with CC. You can make
the stripe two rows wide by knitting with CC for rows 6
and 7.

Bind off, leaving an 8" tail of yarn. Thread yarn through
tapestry needle and sew top seam.

POMPOMS:

Loopy version: With one or both colors held together, wrap
them around a 2 1/2" piece of cardboard (I used my three
fingers instead) about 16-20 times and cut.

Using a strand of MC, tie a knot around the strands to
form a pompom (see how-to with photos on page 15).
Don't cut. Make 2. Attach them to the points on each side
of the top of the hat.

Regular pompoms: Same as above but after you attach
them to the hat cut the loops.

TIES:

Cut 12 strands of yarn 20" long, 6 for each tie.

Thread the six strands through each side of the hat at the
bottom as shown in the picture.

Braid them with 3 sections of two strands each.

Tie a knot at the bottom.

ALTERNATE STYLE FOR TOP OF HAT:

Instead of making one straight seam at the top of the hat, fold the opening into thirds (as shown). Stitch closed using tapestry needle.

You can add pompom's to all three points as I did or not, it looks cute both ways!

I like creating patterns with versatility. This alternate top just gives you another way to make this pattern and give this playtime hat a totally different look!

If you use a bulky yarn as I did this hat will keep its shape nicely. The one shown here was made using Malabrigo Rasta, and the color is Piedras.

Goin' Fishin' Bucket Hat

Materials

Yarn:
MC   Debbie Bliss Donega
Luxury Tweed Chunky

Needles:
US size 13 – 16" circular & dpn

Etc.:
Stitch marker
Tapestry needle

Finished Size:
Newborn 13-14" head

Dreamin' about fishin' with Grandpa! This hat is shown with a real fly - with the hook removed, of course. For a newborn picture this works great, but not for everyday use!

BRIM:

Using size 13 circular needles and MC, cast on 66 stitches. Place marker and join to work in the round.

Row 1: Knit
Row 2: (P1 P2tog) around
Row 3: Knit
Row 4: [(P2, P2tog) (P1, P2tog) 6 times] twice
Next 10 rows: Knit
Row 15: Purl

DECREASE:

Row 16: (K1, K2tog) around
Row 17: Purl
Row 18: (K1, K2tog) around, K2
Row 19: Purl
Row 20: K2tog around

{ Girls' Day out Cloche }

Materials

Yarn:
MC   Pagewood Farms
Hand-dyed Kissi
Color – Meadow
CC   Cha-cha
Color – white

Needles:
US size 13
16" circular & dpn's

Etc.:
Stitch marker
Tapestry needle

Finished Size:
Newborn 13–14" head
6–12 months 16"
18–24 months 18"

This cloche is made to be thick and chunky yet still feminine. The "cha-cha" flower adds that extra little girly touch. Any occasion is the right one for this sweet hat!

HAT:

With size 13 circular needles and MC, holding two strands together, cast on 32 (36, 40) sts. Work in (K1, P1) rib for 1".

Change to size 17 needles and K every row until piece measures 4 ½" (5, 5 ½)

DECREASE:

Row 1 (start 18-24 month size here): (K8, K2tog) around

Row 2: Knit

Row 3: (start 6-12 month size here): (K7, K2tog) around

Row 4: Knit

Row 5 (start newborn size here): (K6, K2tog) around

Row 6 and all even rows (all sizes): Knit

Row 7: (K5, K2tog) around

Row 9: (K4, K2tog) around

Row 11: (K3, K2tog) around

Row 13: (K2, K2tog) around

Row 15: (K1, K2tog) around

Row 17: K2tog around

Cut yarn with 6" tail and pull through remaining sts.

Fold ribbing up over hat.

This forms the bell shaped that makes it a cloche!

FLOWER:

With size 13 circular needles and cha cha, weave on 24 sts.

Turn and P2tog across, 12 sts remaining. Turn work and P2tog across, 6sts remaining.

Using yarn from hat and a tapestry needle, run yarn through remaining sts and attach to hat.

Before cutting yarn, bring tapestry needle and yarn up through center of hat and back twice to make sure flower is securely attached.

{ Pageboy Hat }

Materials

Yarn:
MC   Katia Irish Tweed
Color – #8908 Loden

Needles:
US size 13 – 16"circular & dpn's
US size 17 – 16" circular & dpn's

Etc.:
Stitch marker
Tapestry needle

Finished Size:
Newborn 13–14" head
6–12 months 16"
18–24 months 18"

This hat works for boys and girls and is equally adorable on both! I made this one to look very slouchy but, for a more defined shape, hold two strands together.

HAT:

With size 13 circular needles and MC, loosely cast on 28 (32, 36) sts. Join to work in the round.

Row 1: Knit

Row 2: Purl

Row 3: Knit

Row 4: Purl

Change to size 17 needles

Row 5: (K7 (8, 9) M1) around

Rows 6-13: Knit

DECREASE:

Row 14: (K6, K2tog) around

Row 15: (K5, K2tog) around

Row 16 (start 6-12 month size here): (K4, K2tog) around

Row 17 (start 18-24 month size here): (K3, K2tog) around

Row 18: (K2, K2tog) around

Row 19: (K1, K2tog) around

Row 20: K2tog around

Cut yarn with 6" tail. Using tapestry needle thread yarn through remaining loops.

VISOR:

Pick up and knit 12 (14, 16) sts along cast on edge of hat.

Row 1: K (for size 6-12 months repeat row 1; for size 18-24 months, repeat row 1 twice)

Row 2 (decrease): K2tog, K8 (10, 12), K2tog

Row 3: K2tog, K6 (8, 10), K2tog

Bind off.

{ Little Boy Blue Hat }

Materials

Yarn:
MC   Cascade
Jewel hand dyed
Color - #9282 Aqua

Needles:
US size 13 - 16" circular & dpn's

Etc.:
Stitch marker
Tapestry needle

Finished Size:
Newborn 13-14" head
6-12 months 16"
18-24 months 18"

Little boys need cute hats, too! This hat has a great texture but is still super soft for baby's delicate skin. It has an elongated fit with earflaps that cover little ears and ties for keeping it on his head.

HAT:

Using size 13 circular needles and MC, cast on 30 (35, 40) sts. Join and K every row in the round until piece measures 5" (5 ½, 6)

DECREASE:

Row 1 (start 18-24 month size here): (K6, K2tog) around

Row 2: Knit

Row 3 (start 6-12 month size here): (K5, K2tog) around

Row 4: Knit

Row 5 (start newborn size here): (K4, K2tog) around

Row 6 and all even rows (all sizes): Knit

Row 7: (K3, K2tog) around

Row 9: (K2, K2tog) around

Row 11: (K1, K2tog) around

Row 13: K2tog around

Cut yarn, leaving 6" tail.

Using tapestry needle, thread yarn through remaining loops.

Finish off.

EARFLAPS:

Row 1: Leaving 9 (11, 13) sts in front, pick up and knit 9 sts

Row 2: Purl

Row 3: Knit

Row 4: Purl

Rows 5-7: Repeat Rows 2, 3, &4

Row 8: K2tog, K5 (7, 9), K2tog

Row 6: Purl

Row 7: K2tog, K3 (5, 7), K2tog

Row 8: Purl

Row 9 (last row before i-cord for newborn size): K2tog, K1(3, 5), K2tog

Row 10 (larger sizes only): Purl

Row 11 (last row for 6-12 month size): K2tog, K1(3), K2tog

Row 12 (18-24 month size only): Purl

Row 13: K2tog, K1, K2tog

Using remaining 3 sts, knit i-cord 10" long (or desired length).

POM POMS:

Wrap yarn around a 2-1/2" piece of cardboard (I used my three fingers instead) about 16-20 times. Securely tie a piece of yarn around the bottom of all strands of yarn leaving a 6" tail. Remove yarn from cardboard and secure to hat using the 6" tail of yarn.

Cut loops. Attach it to the top of the hat. For the pompoms at the end of the ties wrap only 8 times for each tie. See how-to section for step by step photographs.

{ Hoodie }

Materials

Yarn:
MC   Cascade
Jewel hand dyed
Color – #9893 Maui Blue

Needles:
US size 15 straight
and 16"circular

Etc.:
Stitch marker
Tapestry needle

Finished Size:
Newborn 13-14" head
6-12 months 16"
18-24 months 18"

Of all my baby knits, this is one of my absolute favorites! It pulls over the baby's head and stays put because of the way the neck portion is made. There are three variations on this one so have fun with it!

HAT:

With size 15 straight needles and MC, cast on 12 (14, 16) sts
Row 1: Knit
Row 2: Purl
Repeat rows 1 and 2 until piece measures 11 (12, 13) inches.
Ending with a knit row, bind off. Fold in half and sew back seam.

NECK:

With size 15 circular needles and right side facing you, pick up
24 (26, 28) sts around bottom of hood and cast on 8 (10, 12) sts.
Place marker and join to work in the round. Work in (K1, P1) rib for
3" (3 ½, 4). Bind off in (K1, P1) rib.

BORDER (around face opening):

Option 1 - plain ribbed border
Pick up 46 (50, 54) sts around face opening. Work in (K1, P1) rib
for 3 rows. Bind off in (K1, P1) rib.
Option 2 - with button
For face ribbing, fold over at the bottom and sew on a big
button.
Option 3 - for ruffle around face opening
Pick up 46 (50, 54) sts around face opening. (K1, M1) in each st
around.
Knit next three rows.
Bind off

POMPOM:

Wrap yarn around a 2 1/2" piece of cardboard (I used my three
fingers instead) about 16-20 times.
Securely tie a piece of yarn around the bottom of all strands of
yarn leaving a 6" tail.
Remove yarn from cardboard and secure to hat using the 6" tail
of yarn.
Cut loops. Attach it to the top of the hat. (See the How-To
section,)

Swaddlers, Costumes, and Photo Props

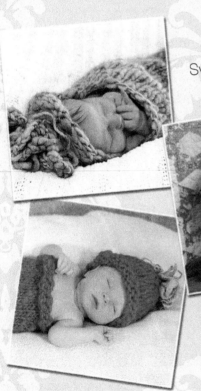

Sweet Pea Pod

Pumpkin Bowl
& Hat

Happy Spring Carrot
Cocoon & Hat

{Swaddlers, Costumes, and Photo Props}

Chili Pepper Cocoon & Hat

Green Bean Cocoon

Little Mermaid Cocoon

{Sweet Pea Pod}

Materials

Yarn
MC Malabrigo Gruesa
Color – Lettuce
(2 skeins)

Needles:
US size 17 – 16"
Circular & dpn's

Etc.:
Stitch marker
Tapestry needle
Spray starch

The first time I did a photo session with this pea pod, my newborn client settled in and fell asleep in seconds, because it was so warm and soft! I would use this for more than just a photo prop. How about a costume or a fun shower gift?

BODY OF POD:

Using size 17 circular needles and MC, cast on 32 stitches.

Place marker and join to work in the round. Knit every row until piece measures 16" or desired length.

DECREASE:

Row 1: (K6, K2tog) around

Row 2 and all even rows: Knit

Row 3: (K5, K2tog) around

Row 5: (K4, K2tog) around

Row 7: (K3, K2tog) around

Row 9: (K2, K2tog) around

Row 11: (K1, K2tog) around

Row 13: K2tog around

With remaining stitches, knit i-cord for four rows.

Cut yarn 6" long and, using a tapestry needle, thread yarn back through remaining stitches.

Finish off.

FOR HOOD:

Pick up and knit 20 stitches from the cast on edge of pod, DO NOT JOIN.

Knit in stockinette stitch (knit one row, purl one row) for 5". End on a purl row (so your next row will be knitting).

Bind off 8 stitches. Knit next 4 stitches onto a dpn.

Bind off remaining 8 stitches.

Using dpn's and the four remaining stitches, knit an i-cord for 3" or desired stem length.

Thread a tapestry needle with yarn, and stitch together the two edges, which you just finished binding off, to form the hood.

LEAF (make 3):

Using size 17 dpn's and MC, cast on 3 stitches
Row 1: Knit
Row 2: Purl
Row 3: M1, K1, M1 (5sts)
Row 4: Purl
Row 5: Knit
Row 6: Purl
Row 7: Knit
Row 8: Purl
Bind off, leaving a 4" tail of yarn.

Attach leaves to each other to form a ring as shown (top photo on opposite page).

Leave the tails of yarn - they will be starched and made to form a coiled spiral.

Using yarn and a tapestry needle, attach leaf ring to top stem. To coil the tails of yarn, I sprayed them with spray starch and wrapped them around my finger as shown (bottom photo on opposite page). If you lay them on a towel,

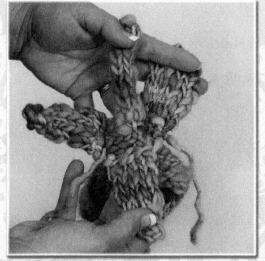

they will dry, but I hurried mine along by using my blow dryer!

Attach leaves to form a ring around the stem with 6" strands of yarn hanging as shown.

Coil the yarn around your finger or a pencil and spray with starch.

Dry using the blow dryer.

Pumpkin Bowl & Hat

Materials

Yarn:
MC   Malabrigo Rasta
Color – Sunset (2 skeins)
CC   Malabrigo Gruesa
Color – Lettuce

Finished Size for hat:
Newborn 13-14" head
6-12 months 16"
18-24 months 18"

Needles:
US size 17 – 16"
circular & dpn's

Etc.:
Stitch Marker
Tapestry Needle
Spray Starch

Whether your child is brand new or sitting up and smiling, this pumpkin set is a great photography prop. It's versatile and super soft, always a must next to baby's skin! Have fun with all the possibilities!

POD:

With size 17 circular needles and MC, cast on 45 stitches.
Work in ribbed pattern (Knit 4, Purl 1), until piece measures 6".

DECREASE:
(Switch to dpn's when needed)
Row 1: (K1, k2tog, K1, P1) around
Row 2, 4, and 6: Knit the Knits and Purl the Purls
Row 3: (K1, K2tog, P1) around
Row 5: (K2tog, P1) around
Row 7: K2tog around
Row 8: Knit around
Cut yarn, leaving a 6" tail. Using tapestry needle, thread yarn
through remaining stitches, bring yarn to inside, and finish off.

HAT:

With size 17 circular needles and MC, cast on 25 (30, 35)
stitches.
Work in ribbed pattern (K4, P1) around. Work until piece
measures 3" (4, 5).

DECREASE:

Row 1: (K1, K2tog, K1, P1) around
Row 2 and 4: Knit the Knits and Purl the Purls
Row 3: (K1, K2tog, P1) around
Row 5: (K2tog, P1) around
Row 6: (K1, P1) around
Row 7: K2tog around
Row 8: K2 tog twice

FOR STEM:

Attach CC leaving a 6" tail and knit and i-cord for 4 rows.
Using CC and tapestry needle, thread yarn through
remaining stitches, take yarn to inside of work,
and finish off.

Take the 6" tail, spray with spray starch, and coil yarn
around your finger or a pencil and let dry (see how-to
photo on page 63). I used my blow dryer to speed up the
drying process.

Happy Spring Carrot Cocoon & Hat

Materials

Yarn:
MC   Malabrigo Gruesa
Color – Glazed Carrot (2 skeins)
CC   Malabrigo Gruesa
Color – Lettuce

Needles:
US size 17 – 16"
circular& dpn's

Etc.:
Stitch Marker
Tapestry Needle

Finished Size Hat:
Newborn 13-14" head
6-12 months 16"
18-24 months 18"

This carrot cocoon can be practical and fun. Dress up your new little bundle in this as a costume or use it as a photo shoot prop. It can also be used for being warm and cozy at home while looking absolutely adorable!

COCOON:

Using size 17 circular needles and MC, cast on 32 sts. Place marker and join to work in the round until piece measures 14" or desired length.

DECREASE:

Row 1: (K6, K2tog) around

Rows 2 and 3: Knit

Row 4: (K5, K2tog) around

Rows 5 and 6: Knit

Row 7: (K4, K2tog) around

Rows 8 and 9: Knit

Row 10: (K3, K2tog) around

Rows 11 and 12: Knit

Row 13: (K2, K2tog) around

Rows 14 and 15: Knit

Row 16: (K1, K2tog) around

Rows 17 and 18: Knit

Row 19: K2tog around

Row 20: Knit

Cut yarn, leaving a 6"tail. Thread tapestry needle and pull yarn through remaining sts. Finish off.

CARROT-TOP HAT:

With size 17 circular needles and MC, cast on 28 (32, 36) sts.

Place marker and join to work in the round. Knit every row until piece measures 4 ½"

DECREASE:

Row 1: (K2, K2tog) around

Row 2: Knit

Row 3: (K1, K2tog) around

Row 4: Knit

Row 5: (K2tog) around

Attach CC and (K1, K2 tog) around.

With remaining sts knit i-cord for 3".

Finish off.

POM POMS:

For the leafy carrot top, make two loopy pom poms using your favorite green yarn. Wrap yarn around a 2 1/2" piece of cardboard (I used my three fingers instead) about 16-20 times. Securely tie a piece of yarn around the bottom of all strands of yarn leaving a 6" tail. Remove yarn from cardboard and secure to hat using the 6" tail of yarn, placing one on each side of the i-cord stem. See how-to with photos on page 19.

{ Chili Pepper Cocoon & Hat }

Materials

Yarn:
MC   Cascade
Jewel Hand Dyed
Color – Scarlett (2 skeins)
CC   Cascade
Jewel Hand Dyed
Color – Highland Green

Finished Size Hat:
Newborn 13-14" head
6-12 months 16"
18-24 months 18"

Needles:
US size 17 – 16"
circular & dpn's

Etc.:
Stitch Marker
Tapestry Needle

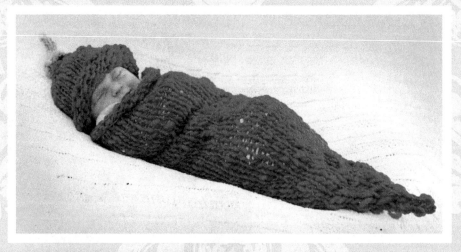

As a costume, swaddle, or just for fun, this spicy little cocoon and hat are adorable! Using the jewel hand dyed makes this cocoon less bulky but still warm.

COCOON:

Using size 17 circular needles and MC, cast on 32 sts. Place marker and join to work in the round until piece measures 14" or desired length.

DECREASE:

Row 1: (K6, K2tog) around

Rows 2 and 3: Knit

Row 4: (K5, K2tog) around

Rows 5 and 6: Knit

Row 7: (K4, K2tog) around

Rows 8 and 9: Knit

Row 10: (K3, K2tog) around

Rows 11 and 12: Knit

Row 13: (K2, K2tog) around

Rows 14 and 15: Knit

Row 16: (K1, K2tog) around

Rows 17 and 18: Knit

Row 19: K2tog around

Row 20: Knit

Row 21-24: Knit i-cord

Cut yarn, leaving a 6"tail.

Thread tapestry needle and pull yarn through remaining sts.

Finish off.

CHILI PEPPER HAT:

Using size 17 circular and MC, cast on 28 (32, 36) sts.

Place marker and join to work in the round until piece measures 5".

DECREASE:

Row 1: (start 18-24 month size here) (K7, K2rog) around

Row 2 and all even rows through row 8: Knit

Row 3: (start 6-12 month size here) (K6, K2tog) around

Row 5: (start newborn size here) (K5, K2tog) around

Row 7: (K4, K2tog) around

Row 9: (K3, K2tog) around

Row 11: (K2, K2tog) around

Row 13: (K1, K2tog) around

Row 15: K2tog around and leave on needles (don't finish off just yet!)

STEM:

With size 13 dpn's and CC, cast on 16 sts.

Row 1: Knit

Row 2: K2tog

Row 3: K2tog, 4sts remain

Join the stem to the hat (knit the red hat sts and green stem sts together as one).

With four green sts remaining, knit i-cord for 8 rows or desired length.

Finish off.

Green Bean Cocoon

Materials

Yarn:
MC   Cascade
Jewel, hand dyed
Color – Highland
Green (2 skeins)

Needles:
US size 17 – 16"
Circular & dpn's

Micellaneous:
Stitch Marker
Tapestry Needle

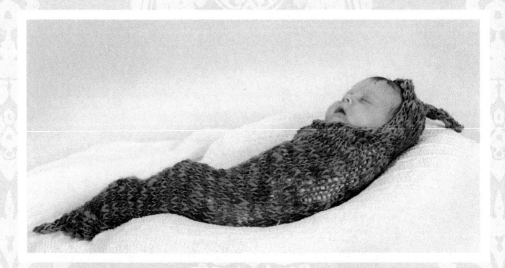

Can't leave this one out of our garden of veggie cocoons!
The beautiful rich green and amazing texture of the Jewel
hand dyed makes this cocoon beautiful to photograph
and, of course, warm and soft for baby.

BODY OF POD:

With size 17 circular needles and MC, cast on 32 stitches.

Place marker and join to work in the round.

Knit every row until piece measures 16" or desired length.

DECREASE:

Row 1: (K6, K2tog) around

Row 2 and all even rows: Knit

Row 3: (K5, K2tog) around

Row 5: (K4, K2tog) around

Row 7: (K3, K2tog) around

Row 9: (K2, K2tog) around

Row 11: (K1, K2tog) around

Row 13: K2tog around

With remaining stitches, knit i-cord for four rows. Cut yarn 6" long and, using a tapestry needle, thread yarn back through remaining stitches.

Finish off.

FOR HOOD:

Pick up and knit 20 stitches from the cast on edge of pod, DO NOT JOIN.

Knit in stockinette stitch (knit one row, purl one row) for 5".

End on a purl row (so your next row will be knitting).

Bind off 8 stitches. Knit next 4 stitches onto a dpn.

Bind off remaining 8 stitches.

Using dpn's and the four remaining stitches, knit an i-cord for 3" or desired stem length.

Thread a tapestry needle with yarn and stitch the two edges that you just finished binding off together to form a hood.

{ Little Mermaid Cocoon }

Materials

Yarn:
MC   Bulky Boucle
Color – Teal (2 skeins)

Needles:
US size 17 – 16"
Circular & dpn's

Etc.:
Stitch Marker
Tapestry Needle

Off to the sea for this mermaid cocoon! I was asked to design this for a children's boutique. We all loved it so much, I decided to add it to this book for everyone to make and enjoy.

COCOON:

Using size 17 circular needles and MC, cast on 32 sts.

Place marker and join to work in the round until piece measures 14" or desired length.

DECREASE:

Row 1: (K6, K2tog) around

Rows 2 and 3: Knit

Row 4: (K5, K2tog) around

Rows 5 and 6: Knit

Row 7: (K4, K2tog) around

Rows 8 and 9: Knit

Row 10: (K3, K2tog) around

FOR TAIL:

Knit next 8 sts onto size 15 straight needles.

INCREASE:

Row 1: P1, M1, P7, M1, turn

Row 2: K1, M1, K9, M1, turn

Row 3: P1, M1, P11, M1, turn

Row 4: K1, M1 K13, M1, turn

Row 5: P1, M1, P15, M1, turn

Row 6: K1, M1, K17, M1, turn

Row 7: Purl these 20 sts on to size 15 circular needles. Pick up the 8 sts from original circular needle and work same increase. The tail will now be knit in four sections and stitched together after finishing.

FIRST TAIL SECTION:

Starting on the end of the stitches that would be the center of the tail as shown here

Working on the right fin with wrong side facing you, Purl 10 sts onto dpn.

Row 1: K2tog, K7, K1, M1, turn
Row 2: P1, M1, P5, (P2tog) twice, turn
Row 3: K2tog, K7, M1, turn
Row 4: P1, M1, P4, (P2tog) twice, turn
Row 5: K2tog, K6, M1, turn
Row 6: P1, M1, P3, (P2tog) twice, turn
Row 7: K2tog, K5, M1, turn
Row 8: P1, M1, P2, (P2tog) twice, turn
Row 9: K2tog, K2, K2tog and bind off remaining 4 sts.

Working on the left fin with right side facing you,
Knit 10 sts onto dpn.
Row 1: P2tog, P7, P1, P1, turn
Row 2: K1, M1, K5, (K2tog) twice, turn
Row 3: P2tog, P7, M1, turn
Row 4: K1, M1, K4, (K2tog) twice, turn
Row 5: P2tog, P6, M1, turn
Row 6: K1, M1, K3, (K2tog) twice, turn
Row 7: P2tog, P5, M1, turn
Row 8: K1, M1, K2, (K2tog) twice, turn
Row 9: P2tog, P2, P2tog and bind off remaining 4 sts.

Work the other side in the same way.

Using a tapestry needle and long strand of yarn,
sew two tail sections together and finish off.

{ Darling Diaper Cover }

Materials

Yarn:
MC   Malabrigo Gruesa
Color – 71 Polygala

Needles:
US size 13 circular
16" circular & dpn's

Etc.:
Stitch Marker
Tapestry Needle
Stitch Holder

Finished Pattern size: Newborn, 6-12 months, 18-24 months

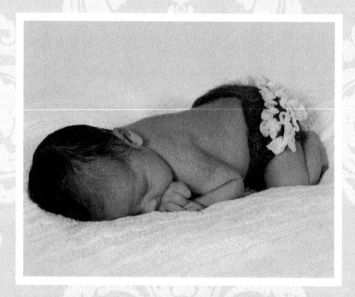

Whether it has ruffles or not, this little cutie offers an adorable way to cover those diapers for both girls and boys! Great for photo sessions, too!

COVER:

Using size 13 circular needles and MC,
cast on 32 (36, 40) stitches.

Work in ribbed pattern (Knit 2 Purl 2),
until piece measures 1 inch.

With Ruffles

After you work (K2, P2), continue as follows:

Rows 1-3: Knit in the round.

Row 4 (and all even rows through row 10): using Cha-Cha, Purl
next 16 (18, 20) stitches. (no Cha-Cha)K next 16(18,20)

Row 5 (and all odd rows through row 11): Knit

Without Ruffles

Knit every round until piece measures 8 (11, 14) inches

For both styles continue as follows:

Row 1: Knit 16 (18, 20) stitches onto a
holder (to work later for back).

Finish knitting row on original needle.

FRONT:

Turn work and continue as follows:

Row 2: P2tog, P2tog, P8 (10, 12), P2tog, P2tog.
12 (14, 16) stitches remain. Turn work.

Row 3: K2tog, K2tog, K4 (6, 8), K2tog, K2tog.
8 (10, 12) stitches remain. Turn work.

Newborn size

Rows 4 and 6: Purl
Rows 5 and 7: Knit
Row 8: Purl.
Bind off.

6-12 and 18-24 month sizes only

Row 4: P2tog, P2tog, P (6, 8), P2tog, P2tog. (10, 12) stitches remain. Turn work

Row 5: K2tog, K2tog, K (4, 6), K2tog, K2tog.

Row 6 (18-24 month size only): P2tog, P2tog, P4, P2tog, P2tog.

Row 7: Knit

Row 8: Purl

Repeat rows 7 and twice. Bind off.

BACK:

Row 1: Pick up stitches from holder and P across 16 (18, 20)

Row 2: Knit

Row 3: Purl

Newborn size

Row 4: K2tog, K12, K2tog

Row 5: P2tog, P10, P2tog

Row 6: K2tog, K8, K2tog

Row 7: P2tog, P6, P2tog

Row 8: Knit

Row 9: Purl

Bind off.

6-12 month size

Row 4: K2tog, K14, K2tog
Row 5: P2tog, P12, P2tog
Row 5: K2tog, K10, K2tog
Row 6: P2tog, P8, P2tog
Row 7: K2tog, K6, K2tog
Row 8: Purl
Row 9: Knit
Row 10: Purl
Bind off.

18-24 month size

Row 4: K2tog, K16, K2tog
Row 5: P2tog, P14, P2tog
Row 6: K2tog, K12, K2tog
Row 7: P2tog, P10, P2tog
Row 8: K2tog, K8, K2tog
Row 9: P2tog, P6, P2tog
Row 10: Knit
Row 11: Purl
Bind off.

All sizes

With tapestry needle, attach front to back.

Yarn Pots

We love to support local artisans!
The yarn pots shown in this book
were handmade by Melanie Mann
Pollon in Woodinville, Washington.
You can contact her at:
revelinclay@hotmail.com or www.etsy.com/shop/revelinclay

They came into my hands via
Carol Gould of Terra Nova Studio
in Duvall, Washington.
Thanks, Carol!

Standard Yarn Weight System

Yarn weight varies from thin to thick and everything in between. The higher the number, the heavier the yarn will be. The heavier the yarn, the fewer stitches per inch.

Yarn weight name & symbol	Lace	Super Fine	Fine
Type of yarn	Fingering	Sock& Baby	Sport
Knit gauge to 4" (stockinette stitch)	33 - 40 sts	27-32 sts	23 - 26 sts
Recommended needle size	0 - 1	1 - 3	3 - 5

Standard Yarn Weight System

In every pattern you knit, a yarn size is recommended. This information is valuable if you want to experiment with yarns other than the one listed on your pattern. After all, we knitters like to play with a variety of yarns whenever we can!

	Light	Medium	Bulky	Super Bulky
Yarn weight name & symbol	3	4	5	6
Type of yarn	DK	Worsted	Chunky	Bulky
Knit gauge to 4" (stockinette stitch)	21 - 24 sts	16 - 20 sts	12 - 15 sts	6 - 11 sts
Recommended needle size	5 - 7	7 - 9	9 - 11	11+

Fiber Company Information

(In order of appearance in book)

Visit your local yarn shop to find these and many more!

Lanaloft: http://brownsheep.com/yarns/lanaloft

Ozark Handspun: http://www.ozarkhandspun.com

Malabrigo Gruesa: http://www.malabrigoyarn.com

Elsebeth Lavold Silky Wool: http://www.knittingfever.com

Cascade Jewel Fiber Design: http://www.cascadeyarns.com

Noro Silk Cotton: http://www.knittingfever.com

Mini Mochi: http://www.straw.com

Debbie Bliss Donegal Luxury Tweed: http://www.knittingfever.com

Pagewood Farms Hand Dyed Kissi: http://www.pagewoodfarm.com

Manos: http://blog.fairmountfibers.com

Trendsetter Chacha: http://www.trendsetteryarns.com

Katia Irish Tweed: http://www.knittingfever.com

Malabrigo Rasta: http://www.malabrigoyarn.com/

Bulky Boucle: http://www.knittingfever.com

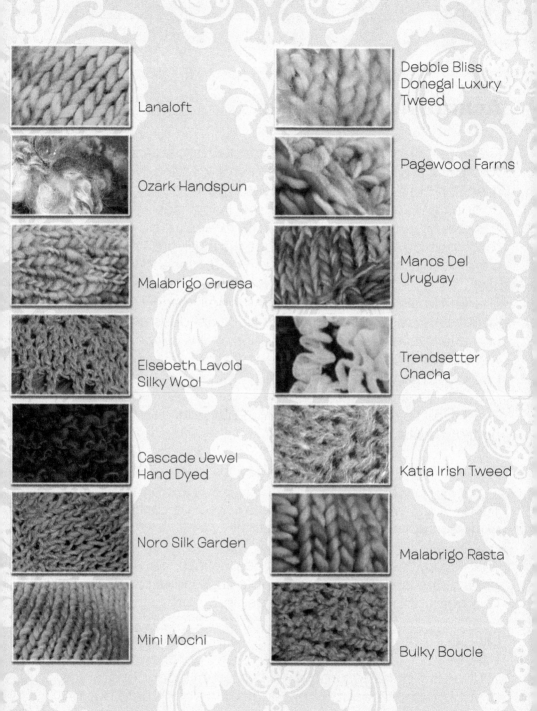

Lanaloft

Debbie Bliss
Donegal Luxury
Tweed

Ozark Handspun

Pagewood Farms

Malabrigo Gruesa

Manos Del
Uruguay

Elsebeth Lavold
Silky Wool

Trendsetter
Chacha

Cascade Jewel
Hand Dyed

Katia Irish Tweed

Noro Silk Garden

Malabrigo Rasta

Mini Mochi

Bulky Boucle

Acknowledgements

First of all, I need to thank my wonderful, patient husband who put up with my endless hours of knitting. Not to mention his tolerance of the "yarn room" that, I think at one time, used to be our formal living room—and the baskets of yarn next to the comfy chairs in the family room and bedroom, too! Without his support, this book never would have happened. I am one, blessed woman!

Thank you also to all of my kiddos who listened to me talk about this book, allowed me to bounce ideas off of them, and even gave me some new ideas in the process. They were so enthusiastic, they even contributed their own two cents to the introduction!

Thank you to my daughter, Annie Ehler, who did the first edit of this book.

Thanks, Mom, for teaching me how to knit!

Thank you, my friends—you all know who you are—for your endless support and cheerleading!

Thank you, thank you, to all of the parents, from coast to coast, who brought their adorable little ones to model for this book. Your support is invaluable.

Last, but not least, thank you to Ozark Handspun for being the first company to support this entrepreneurial knitter with a yarn donation and to all the other fiber companies that have such beautiful products. One can't help but be inspired!

CPSIA information can be obtained
at www.ICGtesting.com
Printed in the USA
LVOW02*2312120816

500047LV00001B/3/P

9 781634 496308